GLIMPSES OF GOD'S LOVE

A Varied Thoughts on Writing Journal

Leenie Brown

Leenie B Books

Halifax

Cover design by Leenie B Books.

ISBNs: 978-1-990607-28-8 (ebook); 978-1-990607-29-5 (paperback); 978-1-990607-30-1 (large print)

www.leeniebbooks.com

CONTENTS

What a Blessing!

———————❤———————

ALMOST FROM THE TIME I could read, I have adored love stories. There is just something about seeing two people in love and learning to work together to find a happily ever after that I find extremely satisfying.

From the time I could read, I have wanted to be an author. The idea of creating characters and fictional worlds was thrilling, and telling stories was always a part of playing for me. And do you know what? When I played, my stuffed animals and dolls went on dates. That's right. I created romance stories for my toys.

Now that I am all grown up, God has granted me my dream of being an author, but not just any author. He has allowed me to become a romance author. How wonderful is that?

Strangely enough, there are some who would look askance at such a question, for they do not approve of romances, and they would almost assuredly not say that writing romance is a gift from God – especially since the romances I write (as Leenie Brown) are not specifically Christian romances or, in other words, romances where faith is an integral element of the story. (I have another pen name, Annilee Nelson, who writes those sorts of romances.)

Sometimes scripture, a mention of Providence, or the Bible will arise in one of my Leenie books since it fits with who a character is. Other times there might not be any mention of anything faith-based at all. However, I can guarantee you that in nearly every story I write, there are glimpses of God's love, and in this journal, I plan to share some of those glimpses with you.

Now, let me ask you one more time – How wonderful is it that God has blessed me with the opportunity and ability to share examples of godly love with the world?

In my opinion, it is a blessing that cannot be adequately measured, and it is my hope that by the end of your journey through this short journal, you'll have begun to see it that way, too.

What's Inside a Leenie Brown Book

Before we dive into seeing how I have written *Glimpses of God's Love* into my catalogue of stories, I thought it would be good to let you know what kind of stories I write. That way, if you decide you'd like to find out more about one of the stories and pick up a book to read – not that you have to or that I expect you to do so, enjoyment of this journal does not depend upon that – you won't be surprised by what is contained inside.

I write Austen-inspired and original sweet Regency romance.

At this point in my writing career, a large portion of my catalogue of stories are written within the Jane Austen universe. These stories play with Miss Austen's characters and plots. Most of these books are based on *Pride and Prejudice*, but not all of them are. I love to delve into creating backstories for and giving happily ever afters to the side characters found in Austen novels, and reforming some of the most unlovable of Miss Austen's characters is a particular delight for me.

In addition to my Austen universe stories, I also have some that are completely original sweet Regency romances. However, despite being Leenie creations, these stories are also kissed with inspiration from many of Jane Austen's novels. It just happens – even when it is not planned.

As stated above, I write sweet romances, but what does that actually mean?

In terms of story tone, you will find that when you read one of my books, the tone of the story is not dark. In fact, it is often quite light and might venture into the made-for-tv rom-com realm. When you finish one of my books, I hope you are left with a sweet sigh and a desire for more. (Kind of like when you get to the end of a favourite sweet treat.)

That being said, I'm talking about more than how a story feels when I use the word *sweet*.

In terms of heat level, I mean that the romance between the main characters is going to focus on the emotional intimacy of my characters and not their physical intimacy. While the story will contain some sexual tension or desire, as is normal between two people who are falling in love and thinking of marrying, none of my books include on-screen physical intimacy. Some might include what are called fade to black moments where you know that physical intimacy is about to happen, but then, the screen goes black.

When taking both story tone and heat level into consideration, if I were to describe my books in a movie rating sort of fashion, I would say that they are all PG-13 or lower. While both the tone and the heat level of my stories are sweet, the obstacles and evil villains in them often aren't and may, at times, be quite bleak and exceptionally evil.

I would also advise you that the PG-13 rating is given because my books often have a more mature theme to them.

What sorts of things might be included that I would qualify as a "more mature theme"? Well, there is abuse in some characters' backstories, there are situations where the main couple is forced to get married because of an indiscretion or compromising situation, and then, there are the stories of reformation that necessitate one or more of the characters having been or being a reprobate at the beginning of the story.

One thing you will never find in my stories is evil triumphing over good. Some villainous characters might "get away with" their behaviours, but they will never succeed in keeping the main couple from finding a way to live happily ever after. Yes, their happily ever afters might actually mean they will have to continue to put up with the Caroline Bingleys, Lady Catherines, and even Wickhams of their world. Because in my writing world...

> *Happily ever after doesn't mean perfect. Even fairytale princesses still have scars after they marry their prince charmings.*

But how can their ever afters be happy if things are not completely calm? It's because love, contentment, and joy are choices, and my main characters will always choose them. That's what makes their ever afters so happy.

Okay, now, that we have that out of the way, let's look at why I think romances are the perfect place to illustrate God's love.

WITHOUT LOVE...

IF I SPEAK IN the tongues of men or of angels, but do not have love, I am only a resounding gong or a clanging cymbal. If I have the gift of prophecy and can fathom all mysteries and all knowledge, and if I have a faith that can move mountains, but do not have love, I am nothing. If I give all I possess to the poor and give over my body to hardship that I may boast, but do not have love, I gain nothing.

1 CORINTHIANS 13:1-3 NIV

The passage above is from 1 Corinthians 13, which is often referred to as the love chapter. It is not uncommon to hear parts of this chapter read at weddings.

"Love is patient. Love is kind..."

Sound familiar?

The portion that is usually read is the part that explains what love is. It's usually presented as a challenge to the couple to develop or maintain those traits of love that are listed in the middle of the chapter.

And when, in this journal, I delve into the glimpses of God's love that are woven into the fabric of my stories, I will highlight those traits and share how they are illustrated by my characters. But before we get to that, I wanted to look at the beginning of the chapter, for here we are told just how important love is.

Without love, we are nothing.

It says that in there three times. It really doesn't matter what wonderful and even miraculous things we do or how good we look to others around us, if we don't have love – God's love – all those things are worthless.

The same is true of a romance story. In romance, love is the essential theme. It <u>must</u> be there. There is no romance without love. It's just how things are. You cannot separate the two.

Can you imagine *Pride and Prejudice* without Mr. Darcy falling ardently in love with Miss Elizabeth, or her sorrow at realizing she might have lost the one man best suited to her in the whole world? I can't – and more precisely, I don't want to! It just wouldn't be the same story.

Sure, the social commentary would still be there, but the tension and drama would be virtually non-existent if there was no threat made by that social commentary on the happy future of our hero and heroine. I suppose you could find some other way to threaten the happiness or livelihood or very life of one or more characters. You could even play on the love a parent has for a child or a sister for a sister or a friend for a friend, and the story would regain its drama. However, it would not be a romance, and again, that's not something I personally would enjoy reading. (Remember, I love romances.)

It is this characteristic of needing love at its core that makes a romance story a great canvas for layering in shades of God's love and illustrating what true-love relationships should look like.

I can hear the nay-sayers saying that the same could be accomplished in any story that had any sort of loving relationship in it, and that's true. However, in the Bible, the relationship between Christ and the church is illustrated as a bride and groom. Therefore, I will maintain my position that romance stories present a uniquely appropriate place to delve deeply into what perfect love – God's love – looks like.

But don't worry. In this journal, I will also have some examples of non-romantic relationships that illustrate this perfect love.

Of course, one must remember that my characters are like you and me – imperfect – and therefore, the examples of love on the following pages will be tainted with that fallibility and perhaps even tinged with sorrow.

Before you turn the page and I present my first story illustration, let me leave you with some weighty words from scripture found in a short verse that highlights just how gravely important love is.

Whoever does not love does not know God, because
God is love. *[1 JOHN 4:8* NIV]

1

In This He Would Not Fail

---❤---

"Lydia." Wickham knelt before her. "I do not have to take you back. No one would condemn me for cutting you loose. But I will not do that. Our children need their mother, and I need my wife. I love you far too much to not care about your behaviour. I have failed you on that account up until now. But this..." He waved the paper before her. "...you have brought upon yourself, and you are the only one who can remove it. Crying about the rain will not make it go away."

Through Every Storm, Chapter 1

If any of you have read or watched *Pride and Prejudice*, you will know that George Wickham and Lydia Bennet are NOT the favourite characters of the story, unless, of course, you are talking about favourite characters to loathe.

Through Every Storm was my first attempt at reforming any of Austen's less-than-loveable characters. My older sister presented me with the idea of trying to make Lydia and Wickham likeable, and I just couldn't resist the challenge. And let me tell you, it was a challenge!

But tackling the intriguing task set before me by writing *Through Every Storm* was also when I fell in love with taking an unworthy, ne'er-do-well sort of character and changing them into a character who tugged at my heartstrings and wormed their way into my affections.

But God demonstrates his own love for us in this: While we were still sinners, Christ died for us. [ROMANS 5:8 NIV]

It was in writing these sorts of stories where I first got to contemplate God's love for me and learned to visualize the above verse in a way I hadn't done before. Now, I'm not saying that what I was doing in my stories was equal to what God did/does for us. Nobody is equal to God!

I know that my writings are just a tiny fragment of a glimpse of the love He has for me – and you. But sometimes, a small glimpse of something much larger settles in our minds just how enormous the larger thing is.

In this story of mine, Wickham is a very flawed picture of the love in Romans 5:8, but the principle is there. Stay with me here and let me see if I can explain it.

The plot of the book in a nutshell is that Lydia has left her home, children, and husband to travel to Derbyshire to visit her sister, Elizabeth Darcy. She's done this because she needs some money, and, well, Elizabeth married very well.

Lydia has taken the precaution to be escorted on her journey by one of the soldiers stationed near her home in Newcastle, but she hasn't thought out how that might look to everyone – including her husband. She also hasn't discussed her plan with him at all.

She has just left.

Lydia has acted stupidly. She is in the wrong and has made a rather large mess of things. Her intentions were not all bad, but her execution of her desires was.

The book opens with Wickham drowning his sorrows at a pub. (I did mention he's a flawed character, right?)

Thankfully, he has a good friend and brother-in-law, Colonel Denny, who is not about to let him pickle himself with alcohol when his children need him and he still has a hope of winning his wife back.

Convinced of what he must do, Wickham gathers his fortitude and tracks down his wife. Why does he do this? Is it just to save face in the community? Is it to make sure his children have a mother?

No.

His motivation is love.

No one would have expected it, but against the odds, Wickham loves his wife most ardently. So strong is that love for her that he's willing to sacrifice himself and do the hard work both to restore their marriage and family to something better than what it has always been and to help Lydia grow into the woman she needs to be.

It's a rough, painful road. I wrote this story with a box of tissues at my side because I had to delve into my characters' feelings. I had to feel Lydia's hurt and longing as well as the fear each of them hid inside themselves at the thought of losing the one they love most.

Can you see the flicker of comparison between God sending Jesus to die for us while we were still wandering and filthy with sin when we didn't deserve it and Wickham tracking down his wife and providing a way for her to be restored to him when he didn't have to take her back?

I hope you can, and like I said, it's just a flicker. It's just a glimpse of God's pure, holy, and sacrificial love for us. But then, all that human relationships can ever give us is a peek at perfect love.

The characteristics of God's perfect, sacrificial love are what are detailed in 1 Corinthians 13. And the first on the list is patience. God's perfect love is long-suffering. It is willing to endure.

Willingness to endure is one of the things that George Wickham is going to have to have if he is going to be successful in his quest to reclaim his marriage, and, let me tell you, he has it. He is firmly determined to be successful, for he knows far too well the devastating results of failure.

———

Lydia stirred next to him and tilted her head to look up at him. "What has you looking so desolate, my dear?"

"I was thinking of my father and mother."

She squeezed him tightly. He had told her the story of his parents. "I love you, Mr. Wickham."

He smiled down at her. "And I love you, Mrs. Wickham. There is nothing you can do that will ever change that." **He would not fail her** *as his father had failed his mother. He would endure the pain of love when it came and would fight to reclaim the wonderful, comforting feeling it afforded him as he sat here with her wrapped in his embrace, her lips pressed against his.*

THROUGH EVERY STORM, CHAPTER 10

———

This closing excerpt for this first journal entry is from the final chapter of Wickham and Lydia's story, and as you can see, he seems to have patiently endured through the storm in which he found himself and has successfully restored his marriage. (I'd label that a spoiler, but this is romance – happily ever after is expected, so his success should not surprise you.)

And I'd say with great certainty that the promise below, which he made to his wife in Darcy's study at Pemberley at the beginning of this tale, is one he will move heaven and earth, as far as a mere mortal is able to do, to keep.

*Through every storm of
life, I shall love you.
Yours forever, George*

2

The Kindness of a Father

---❤---

The kindness in the man's eyes caused Miles to pause before returning his appreciation of the offer. Mr. Wesley's expression was one that he had never seen in his own father's eyes. He had witnessed the kindness with which some of his friends had been treated by their fathers, but until this moment, he had not felt the warmth that such a thing could bring to a soul in quite the way he had just experienced it. While Mr. Wesley was not clapping him on the shoulder and welcoming him to the family, he was also not throwing him out. It was almost as if the man wished for Miles to succeed in the quest placed before him.

Standing on the drive next to his carriage, Miles turned halfway and looked back at the flat façade of the Wesleys' home with its three rows of symmetrical windows. Had anyone ever left the fate of his welcome to his own efforts?

His Sensible Heart, Chapter 1

In a typical, loving family, parents are kind to their children. They provide what is needed without any expectation of their provision bringing some sort of benefit for themselves. We do not, normally, comfort babies, feed them, clothe them, etc. and expect them to settle their tab once their allowance starts rolling in. Such a scenario seems absurd to most of us.

However, in Miles Chapman's experience, what we might think of as normal is not the norm because, you see, his father, Sir Allen, is a narcissist of the cruelest variety. Nothing in Sir Allen's life is allowed to make him appear any less fabulous than he thinks he should. If that means destroying the career of the man his daughter loves but of whom he does not approve, so be it. If it means starting rumours to ruin the reputation of the lady his youngest son loves but of whom he also does not approve, well, then, the tales must be manufactured and spread.

When I said, "The obstacles and evil villains in them (my stories) often aren't (sweet) and may, at times, be quite bleak and exceptionally evil," in the journal entry about what you could expect to find in a Leenie book, I wasn't overstating things. Sir Allen and the trouble he causes is one example that highlights the truth of my words.

Thankfully, both his son and his daughter find help from others who exemplify the verse:

Love is kind. [*1 CORINTHIANS 13:4B NIV*]

For Miles's sister, Belle, it is their aunt. (Belle's story can be found in *His Irreplaceable Belle*.) For Miles, it is Mr. Wesley, the father of the lady he loves and wishes to marry.

Unfortunately for Miles, he has grown up in his own father's shadow and has only ever been expected to be popular and make his dad look good, and Charlotte Wesley isn't the sort of girl who wants to date or marry a guy who is so full of himself.

But the thing is, Miles isn't as consumed by his own appearance as his father is. Miles has been focused on pleasing his father and having a good time – until he met Charlotte and his father started rumours about her. That's when he finally saw his father for the horrible person he was and broke ties with him.

Oh, my! The trouble that Miles's determination to do what was right brings to him. It starts with a removal of his inheritance and deteriorates as the strictures his father attempts to put in place do not work to separate Miles from Charlotte.

Sir Allen is the antithesis of "love is kind."

Mr. Wesley, on the other hand, is just the sort of gentleman Miles needs in his life. He's not going to willingly hand over his daughter's future to Miles even though it would save Charlotte's reputation. He is intent on seeing both of his daughters happily married and in loving situations, and at the start of the story, a marriage between Miles and Charlotte does not appear to be one which would result in what Mr. Wesley wants. You see, Charlotte does not like Miles (or so she says), and Mr. Wesley has heard all about Miles's reputation.

Let's pause here for a moment and have a little word study.

When I looked up the Greek word *love* that is used in 1 Corinthians 13:4, which I found on biblehub.com, I discovered that that particular word is only used once in scripture – in this verse. I was kind of hoping I could find other examples of how it was used in the Bible to help me get a deeper, clearer understanding of the word.

Since I could not find it used in scripture, I went to Google and started searching the meaning and synonyms for kind. Words that kept coming up in my search results were *compassionate*, *benevolent*, and *charitable*.

Ah! I thought. *Charity. That's the word that was used rather than love in the King James version of the Bible from which I was taught as a child. I'll look that word up to see if it helps me since results for kind seem well connected to it.*

To that end, I opened *Johnson's Dictionary Online* in a new browser tab and looked up the word *charity.* This is a digitized version of Samuel Johnson's 1755 dictionary, and because it is such an old dictionary, I figured it would get me closer to what the word charity meant when the KJV Bible was translated since, as I'm sure we are all aware, the meaning and usage of words changes over time.

Here is what I found for the entry: *charity.*[1]

1. *Tenderness; kindness; love*

2. *Goodwill; benevolence; disposition to think well of others*

3. *The theological virtue of universal love*

To me, those definitions described Mr. Wesley quite well, and here is where this small word study connects back to what we were talking about before.

As you can see in the story excerpt at the beginning of this entry, Mr. Wesley does not just send Miles away. He sees the promise of who Miles might actually be behind his façade, and he's disposed to think well of the young man and give him a chance to prove himself – which, by the way, Miles does in a fashion that surprises everyone around him. Mr. Wesley was right. Miles had great potential.

Now, as I said, at the beginning, kindness does not express itself to gain something in return. It is charitable and benevolent just because that is what it is. There is no external motivation for the goodwill charity (aka love) expresses. And that information might cause you to wonder if Mr. Wesley can be used as an example of love being kind. Isn't he hoping to receive something from Miles in return, such as improvement?

Perhaps.

But even this wish is not motivated by Mr. Wesley's own desires to please himself so much as it is to possibly be able to present an excellent husband for his daughter at the end of his agreement with Miles. So, it can't be completely separated from some joy or pleasure being received by the extender of the kindness. The nuanced difference comes in the motivation of the benefactor, and in this case, Mr. Wesley's motivation is his daughter's happiness and his genuine care for the young man who says he loves her.

And what are the results of the kindness Mr. Wesley bestows upon Miles? Well, this is a romance, so you know that there will be a happy ending for Miles and Charlotte, and therefore, a pleased father because his daughter will be cherished as he wants her to be. But beyond that, for Miles, the result is something deeper and even more personal. He has been blessed with the best tutor from whom to learn how a gentleman and father should be, and through this course of study, Miles would claim one of the greatest desires of his heart, for...

...he would be thought of and spoken about as what
he had longed to be, a good man.

---

1. A Dictionary of the English Language, by Samuel Johnson, 1755, "charity, n.s," Accessed 2022/10/22. "charity, n.s."

3

When Good Intentions Go Bad

"ARE YOU CERTAIN THIS is what you want?"

Langley turned away from Lady Matlock to find Mr. Bennet observing him with great interest and a hint of compassion. He allowed himself to glance at Kitty. Her cheeks were flushed, and her jaw was firmly set. She did not look at all pleased with how things had progressed this morning. However, he did not know why she should look so stricken. This was what she wanted. She had made it perfectly clear yesterday that she had no intention of marrying him. One would have to be excessively stupid to misconstrue "I am not marrying him" to mean anything other than the lady had no desire to be his wife.

He nodded as he turned back to her father. "It is." This lie did not fall any easier from his lips than any of the others had so far today.

"Well, then, Mr. Langley, if things can be kept quiet, I will absolve you of any duty to my daughter. However, if you change your mind..."

Langley clamped his teeth together tightly and gave a sharp nod of his head before looking at Miss Bennet one final time and leaving the room and any hope for a happy future behind him.

CHERISHING KITTY, PROLOGUE

As you read the above excerpt, did you wonder why in the world I have chosen this book to include in a collection of stories that give glimpses of God's love?

I mean...

How does breaking up demonstrate anything about God's love? Especially when the hero is lying while doing it?

Stick with me. I assure you I have a good reason.

In fact, if you make note of the bold words above and the ones in the verse below, you might discover that reason.

*[Love] does not dishonor others, **it is not self-seeking**, it is not easily angered, it keeps no record of wrongs. [1 CORINTHIANS 13:5 NIV]*

Still wondering? Let me explain.

Compromises and forced marriages are common Regency romance tropes. Courting missteps, such as being caught kissing a fellow you fancy, are no small thing in this era.

Such a transgression would tarnish a Regency miss's reputation, and the Regency gentleman's honour would be called into question for his part in their breach of propriety. If he were of noble character, he would redeem the situation by offering for the young lady, and, should all parties agree, the two would marry.

In the final chapter of *Persuading Miss Mary*, the book that comes right before *Cherishing Kitty* in my *Marrying Elizabeth* series, Kitty and Lorcan (aka Mr. Langley) were caught kissing. Passionately. In the music room during her sister's wedding breakfast.

There was some discussion in the music room about marriage, during which Kitty declared she was not marrying Lorcan. After this, it was reasoned that since only family members and perhaps a servant or two witnessed the incident, there was a chance that things could be kept quiet, preventing any damage to Kitty's reputation or Lorcan's honour.

A meeting, which would include several of the people in the music room, as well as the father of the lady whose reputation hung in the balance and the gentleman who was being held responsible for the kissing that was interrupted, was set for the morning.

This is the backdrop to the prologue of Kitty and Lorcan's story.

As you've read in the excerpt above, instead of doing what many would consider the right and honourable thing to do, Lorcan declares he does not want to marry Kitty. It's a lie, but he thinks he is giving her what she wants even if it will leave him heartbroken and with an inky black stain on his honour.

What Lorcan does not know is that Kitty had a reason for her declaration in the music room that had nothing to do with actually *not* wanting to marry him and everything to do with honouring a promise to a dear friend.

She had expected to get time to speak to Lorcan after things were concluded in the music room at the end of the previous book, but she didn't get that chance.

So, to summarize, we have both a hero and a heroine who are doing exactly what 1 Corinthians 13:5 says – "love is not self-seeking" – and the results are a disaster. How can that be? Surely, if one follows what the scripture says, one's life should be perfect, right?

chuckles and wishes it were true

My dear reader, perfection only exists in heaven. We might try to get close here on earth, but our lives are never going to be perfect. Humans err – a lot and often. And our hero and heroine, though not real humans, are just as imperfect as any of the rest of us are.

What's the human error here?

There are two: assumption and lack of communication.

Kitty and Lorcan are never given time to have a heart-to-heart conversation, which could clear up the misunderstanding quite easily. And rather than ask to speak privately to Kitty, during which he could present himself as a gentleman who loves her and wants to marry her, Lorcan just assumes that it will do no good and that he's putting her wishes ahead of his desires.

I'm sure that never happens in real relationships, does it? *chuckles again*

We all communicate with those we love perfectly, and we never assume their thoughts, do we? *still chuckling*

I'm pretty sure that I'm not the only one who has fallen prey to those things.

To answer before listening – that is folly and shame. [PROVERBS 18:13 NIV]

Lorcan has answered before listening – though to be fair, he thinks he has heard enough, and Kitty has not said anything to let him know there is anything more to say.

For her part, Kitty hears his reply here and assumes he never really loved her as she thought he did.

Oh! That's a lot of assuming and things that need to be said but aren't!

All this non-listening and jumping to conclusions in the story leads to a lot of hurt and pain. With things muddled and messy, Lorcan leaves town and returns to his home while Kitty is required to return to Longbourn and miss the remainder of the season because of her indecorous behaviour. Both lovers wile away their time with broken hearts that could have been avoided.

This leads us naturally to ask:

How does one resolve a misunderstanding based on assumption and miscommunication or, more accurately in this case, assumption and complete lack of communication?

The answer is both simple to know and hard to do.

One communicates.

That is a simply obvious answer is it not? But how does one say, "Wait a minute. I love you. I didn't say all I needed to say. Can we talk about this?" when one is convinced that the person you love does not love you? That's hard – and risky – and takes a great deal of bravery.

Or in this case, maybe it just takes a Regency-era "flat tire."

———

"Ho! A carriage!" one of the grooms cried.

Lorcan turned to look toward Meryton. There indeed was a carriage coming toward them. He rubbed his sore head again and sent a prayer heavenward that the carriage was not Mr. Bennet's.

"Are you in need?" the coachman from the approaching carriage called.

"We have a broken wheel," the groom shouted back.

The carriage with four good wheels drew to a stop, and Lorcan's groom joined one of the carriage's grooms in speaking to someone inside the carriage. Lorcan moved closer so that he could hear what was being said.

"We cannot carry our passengers. They will need a place to rest," his groom was saying.

"Of course, we can assist," came the reply from inside the carriage.

Then, to Lorcan's delighted surprise, Charles Bingley stepped out of the vehicle. Lorcan could manage spending a bit of time with Bingley – even if it did require him to also spend time with Kitty's eldest sister who was now Mrs. Bingley.

"Langley," Bingley cried. "It is very good to see you." Though the man wore a smile, he glanced nervously back at his carriage. "I believe we have room for – is it two passengers?"

"Yes, and a place for a groom."

Bingley nodded. "That is absolutely doable." He looked at the groom who had hailed his carriage. "See that Mr. Langley and—"
He looked at Lorcan.

"Alfred Langley, my cousin," Lorcan supplied.

"See that both Mr. Langleys' things are transferred. We have several empty rooms just waiting to be occupied." Again, he cast a nervous look toward his carriage.

"We can stay in Meryton," Lorcan offered.

"Nonsense. I am sure we will get on just fine at Netherfield." He sounded confident, but there seemed to be hesitance in his expression.

"Are you certain?"

"Yes, yes. I am sure it will all work out as it should."

CHERISHING KITTY, CHAPTER 2

And it will work out as it should, but not without some difficulty. Pride and hurt feelings can make things challenging. Admitting one's fault or regret is never painless.

But then, love is not for the faint of heart.

"Kitty, please," he begged.

Her heart sighed its desire at his use of her Christian name. It had always sounded so much sweeter falling from his lips than anyone else's.

"What did you mean? What do you regret?"

She blew out a breath and willed herself not to run away instead of answering. Dread filled her now just as it had when he had asked her about her regret in the garden. She still remembered his kiss fondly. She dreamt of it nearly every night. Its memory caused her to cry into her pillow. But more painful than the recollection of that sweet stolen moment was the loss of everything which had come before it.

"I regret allowing you to kiss me." She tried to keep her eyes on him. However, it was too difficult, and she looked away just as she had in the garden.

"Why?" The question she had expected him to ask her in the garden came in a whisper.

"Because..." she shrugged. How did one put this into words? "So much was lost because of it."

He took a step closer to her. "What was lost?"

Again, she blew out a breath and willed herself not to turn and run. "Us. Our friendship."

He took her hands, gripping them as tightly as one might do to keep someone from falling from a precipice.

The door below them opened.

"I must go," she pulled on her hands.

"But you refused me."

"And you refused me," she replied, once again giving her hands a tug. This time he released them.

"Why?" he asked.

She shook her head. "I must go. It would not do to have my sister find us here like this." She turned away from him.

He followed her two steps down the hallway. "You are not going to stay in your room until I am gone, are you?"

"No. Jane would never allow it."

"But do you want to?"

She stopped and nodded without turning around. "It would be easier."

"Easier than what?" he pressed.

She looked over her shoulder at him. "It would be easier than being reminded of what was lost." Even if it had been a foolish fantasy, and he had not loved her as she thought he had.

"I will go see if Lori is still here and has not wandered off to Meryton." Mr. Alfred Langley's voice floated up the stairs.

"Were you going to Meryton?" Kitty asked.

"I considered it." He looked nervously down the stairs. She knew just as he did that, soon, his cousin would make the turn at the next landing and discover them.

"Why?" she whispered.

"You should go to your room." He turned to go in the opposite direction.

"Why?" she whispered again. This time more earnestly.

He stopped and turned back towards her. "For the same reason you would rather stay in your room. Now, go before he sees us. He can be insufferable. Perhaps we can discuss this more later?"

Kitty nodded as, for the first time in more than a month, a real, happy smile spread from her heart to her lips. Perhaps it had not been such a foolish fantasy after all.

CHERISHING KITTY, CHAPTER 5

And discuss it later, they do. Eventually. When they can finally catch a few minutes to speak privately. (He wasn't kidding when he said his cousin could be insufferable. LOL)

As they work through the item standing in the way of their marrying, Kitty and Lorcan discover that it takes a good bit of fortitude to carve out and maintain a happily ever after.

Just like us when we're building a loving relationship – whether that is in a marriage or a friendship – Kitty and Lorcan will have to be vulnerable and trusting. They will have to cling to patience and reshape expectations. It will require forgiveness and perseverance.

But the prize for doing so? Ah, that prize is so very worth the effort.

4

WHAT LOVE DID

———❤———

"FINDING ONE'S FOOTING IN society can be a challenge, especially for someone who has parentage that the elite of society deems undesirable. You said as much today."

Caroline shrugged and lifted her chin. She would not retaliate. Her father was a tradesman, but he was well-respected. He was not disparaging her father. He was stating a fact. Despite her efforts to calm herself, her heart raced and that dreaded feeling of tears forming would not go away.

"To look at you..." He shook his head. "You are beautiful, but to know you?" His eyes swept from her head to her toes and back. "Good heavens, I wish you were as kind as you are beautiful."

That was a step too far, and Caroline could not contain her anger any longer.

"How dare you," she spat. "Who placed you in a position to reprimand me on anything?" She stepped closer to him, her eyes narrowing.

"No one," he replied. "Just me." He left his place of repose against the door and matched her advance with a step of his own. Did she always smell of oranges and spice? The scent fit her.

She lifted a brow. "Why?"

He blew out a breath. "I'll be hanged if I know." He had attempted to keep his thoughts to himself, but for some reason he felt compelled to see her improve, to reach her potential. It was likely that glimpse of her thoughtful, quiet nature at breakfast which had done it.

She shook her head in bewilderment. He was making little sense. How could he not know why he thought it his place to admonish her?

He stepped to the side so that the door was free, but he once again caught her arm as she moved past him. Pulling her close, he whispered, "You are a beautiful, accomplished young woman who does not need to belittle others to make herself look better."

Then, before he could do something foolish like make use of the kissing bough which hung just in front of the door, he released her.

ONE WINTER'S EVE, CHAPTER 4

For those of us who are well acquainted with *Pride and Prejudice*, one character's name might immediately spring to mind when words such as envious and self-seeking are mentioned. That name is Caroline Bingley. She is, of course, the younger sister of Mr. Darcy's best friend and is very eagerly and actively seeking to make a match with Mr. Darcy. For that reason, she is not welcoming of Miss Elizabeth and is quite obviously jealous.

For a writer of Austen-inspired romances, Caroline is a fun character to play with when writing variations and adaptations. Many authors will make her much more menacing than Jane Austen ever did. (That seems to be a favourite way to deal with her.) And then, there's me.

I've used her as an antagonist to cause some substantial trouble, but I've also found it fun to pull out a completely opposite side of her and turn her into a more sympathetic character.

One Winter's Eve is the first time I tried to "reform" her. I love the resulting story, and the challenge of writing *Pride and Prejudice's* "mean girl" as an injured lady who has lost her way was delightful.

You may be asking why I would include a character like Caroline in this journal when she so obviously lacks the qualities of godly love found in the following verses:

[4] *Love is patient, love is kind. **It does not envy**, it does not boast, it is not proud. [5] It does not dishonor others, **it is not self-seeking**, it is not easily angered, it keeps no record of wrongs.* [*1 CORINTHIANS 13:4-5 NIV*]

Well, that's an easy answer. It's because it's love (or the process of falling in love) that opens her eyes to her faults and helps her overcome these deficiencies of character.

In the excerpt above, you met the man who is going to point out Caroline's undesirable behaviour and help her see her good qualities. This man (who is, whether he wants to be or not and whether he knows it or not, in love with Caroline) is none other than Darcy's cousin, Colonel Richard Fitzwilliam.

The colonel has a no-nonsense sort of approach to many things in life. He speaks plainly, even when others don't want him to, and he takes action where others might hold back. It is these qualities, combined with his finely-honed observation skills, that help him be just the right person to help Caroline improve.

———

"Now, about Miss Bingley."

Richard's brows furrowed. "What about her?"

"It is unlike you to spend any amount of time with her. In fact, you usually attempt to avoid her at all costs."

"There have been few others around."

Darcy's brow rose. Skepticism suffused his face.

Richard shrugged. "I needed something with which to occupy my time. So, I have been attempting to understand her."

Skepticism changed to amusement as Darcy shook his head.

"It is not my fault that your betrothed put the notion in my mind." He folded his arms and leaned back in his chair. "I think I have figured her out – Miss Bingley that is."

"You have?"

Richard nodded. "I have. She wants improvement in a few areas, so I have set myself to the task."

"And this is that with which you have decided to occupy yourself? Improving Caroline Bingley?"

Richard chuckled. "Whether she wishes it or not."

ONE WINTER'S EVE, CHAPTER 6

Is he successful?

Here's a little peek at the answer to that question.

"You have trusted me with your story about Mr. Wickham, so I feel I can trust you with this." She waited to get an assurance from Georgiana. "I have not told anyone – Louisa would not understand. She never felt Father's displeasure as greatly as I did." She drew a breath. "One thing my father said to me over and over when I would return home from school for a holiday was that no matter how many accomplishments I acquired, there was truly only one that mattered." She looked down at the bed cover and smoothed the wrinkles with her hand. "Kindness." She sighed heavily. "It has been pointed out to me that I have not been as kind as I should be. Oh, I knew I was not being kind, but it is so much easier to not feel like a pebble among jewels when one chooses to point out the failings of another instead of noticing her own. Eventually, a practice becomes a habit and a habit, a way of life, unless someone forces you to look at yourself in a different light — not as wanting but as accomplished."

Georgiana smiled. "Richard?"

Caroline nodded. **"He has not ignored my faults but sees my abilities despite those faults."**

ONE WINTER'S EVE, CHAPTER 10

Isn't that what God does? He loves us despite our sin. He sees our potential to be what He has designed us to be, but He also won't ignore our shortfalls. He patiently works on us to draw us to Himself and to form us into the masterpieces He desires us to be.

It is this sort of godly love that Richard is demonstrating to Caroline that has helped her see where she needs to improve. She knows she has fallen short of what her father taught her to be – of the sort of lady her father would be proud to know she has become.

As she faces this shortcoming and learns that she is capable of being so much more than she has been, her actions begin to change to reveal her true character, and by the end of the book, she's well on her way to being a lady who is capable of taking her place in good society and who has put away envy and her self-seeking ways. She is secure in who she is, and ready to stand at her colonel's side, graciously welcoming one and all. It is a transformation that really would not have been possible without the wonderful, though sometimes trying, outworking of love in her life, for...

> *Her character had been sadly wanting for some time and might have still been wanting had it not been for a particular, persistent, annoying, demanding colonel.*

5

TO FORGIVE A FRIEND

———— ♥ ————

"Do you hate him?" Georgiana tilted her head as she always did when studying something closely.

Darcy returned to his seat. Speaking of his thoughts and feelings was not something he had ever enjoyed doing, but he knew the look on his sister's face. She would have an answer either now or sometime in the future. And since it seemed better to have it over and done with, he expelled a breath, shook his head, and began.

"I do not know. I have hated him. Every time I have stood in a ballroom or sat at a musicale or wandered the museum and watched the happiness of the people around me, I have despised him." He shrugged. *"But happiness has found me at last, despite Bingley's interference, and now I am unsure how to think of him."* He blew out a great breath, hoping that some of his uncertainty would leave him with it. *"I suppose some would say I should forgive him while others would have me shun him. I am unsure I can*

do either. He is married to Elizabeth's sister, so refusing to see him
would harm her, and that I will not do. However —"

FINALLY MRS. DARCY, CHAPTER 2

As I said in the introduction to this journal, not all the entries that I have selected to include will be about romantic relationships. This, just like the one about kindness, is one of those non-romantic love journal entries. This one deals with love between friends.

"...it (love) keeps no record of wrongs." [1 CORINTHIANS 13:6 NIV]

Step into your imagination with me and visualize the following scenario. You, as a teenage girl, are at your part-time job, talking with your co-worker because it's a slow night. You talk about all sorts of things: school, the future, that party you both heard about that got broken up by the cops, and eventually, boys. During this conversation, you happen to share that you find a certain boy in your class attractive. You think nothing of this conversation until a few days later, when a note is intercepted by the teacher and read aloud.

That's when you discover that your co-worker has shared your appreciation of that certain boy you mentioned with a friend and that friend has decided to share that information with her friend via a note – the very one that the teacher is reading to your class, which also happens to be that cute boy's class.

Somehow, you don't melt into the floor or die from mortification, and you leave the class under your own power ready to vent and cry about your anger and humiliation to your best friend. Thank goodness it was the last class of the day!

Venting helps. You get all the immediate emotions out, and by the time you once again have to see your co-worker at work or school, you're ready to pretend that all is well. You put on your pleasant smile, zip up your be-nice hoodie, and proceed with life, all while anger and hurt bubble below the surface.

Friends can hurt us, and they can make us mad – even when you're Mr. Darcy.

The premise of Finally Mrs. Darcy is based on one friend injuring another.

The first time a wound was inflicted upon Mr. Darcy and Mr. Bingley's friendship was six years before this story starts, and it was Darcy who had injured Bingley through secretly helping to separate him from the lady he loved.

The second time an injury happened between the two friends was five years before the story starts, and it was Bingley's response to Darcy's confession of wrongdoing which caused the damage.

Notice in the excerpt above that Darcy lists two possible responses to being injured – forgiveness or shunning.

Bingley, when he discovered the wrong Darcy had done to him, chose the second option – shunning. He severed their friendship completely. For five years, Darcy has been hoping that Bingley will relent, and that their relationship could be restored, but it has not happened.

That's where I, as the storyteller, step in and arrange things so that the two will be thrust together and forced to resolve the issue that lies between them in some fashion. This is where Darcy is in the excerpt above. He knows he's going to have to face Bingley at some point and is uncertain how he is going to proceed when it happens.

However, when Bingley finally presents himself to his friend, Darcy will discover that he knows without hesitation exactly how to respond, for his actions will be motivated by and grounded in love. That's not to say the confrontation does not transpire without some flaring tempers and harsh words, but the end result of the conversation will be the start of a new beginning between them.

———

"I cannot say how we will move on from here, but it shall not be done separately." Darcy stood and extended his hand to Bingley. "I once told you that my good opinion once lost was lost forever; however, that is not true. Although you may have lost it for a time, that does not mean it cannot be restored with time and effort."

Bingley gripped Darcy's hand tightly and gave it a firm shake. "Thank you. I shall endeavour to deserve it."

FINALLY MRS. DARCY, CHAPTER 6

———

According to 1 Corinthians 13:6, love doesn't keep an account of wrongs. In other words, love forgives.

That sounds simple, but it is often the furthest thing from simple that anything could be. There are all sorts of emotions – natural responses – that must be worked through. There are consequences that must be faced. Things are not going to go back to how they were. They can't. The fabric of life has been forever altered.

Sometimes relationships cannot and should not be restored even though forgiveness is offered. For example, if the person who has committed the wrong has died, the relationship cannot be restored. Or if the person presents a danger, the relationship should not be restored.

However, the circumstances in this story are not such that Darcy and Bingley cannot or should not pursue a restoration of their friendship. They will eventually become good friends again, but that does not mean that what transpired between them somehow miraculously disappears as if it never happened. It doesn't.

———

"He has survived well," Darcy commented. It was not the first time he had said so since Richard's arrival.

"I am sure there are shadows," Elizabeth replied. "There always are."

Darcy clasped her hand in his. He knew she was not only speaking of shadows formed by the atrocities of war but also of the

shadows that hung about any individual after a trying experience
— fears, guilt, regrets, or the dreaded expectation of the recurrence
of some event.

"They can be vanquished," he whispered.

Her head rubbed against his shoulder as she nodded. "Most can,
but I imagine there are particularly dark ones which cannot." She
squeezed his hand. "I am glad that no such shadows have attached
themselves to our family."

"As am I." He shifted slightly as his foot began to prickle from
sitting in one position for so long. "I fear the shadow over Bingley
may never rise."

Elizabeth smiled and lifted his hand to her lips. "You are a very
good man, Mr. Darcy."

"Thank you." He turned his head to look down at her. "But I am
not entirely certain as to the reason for my goodness."

"You care for him." She smiled up at Darcy and tilted her head
toward where Bingley and Jane sat listening to Richard's tale. "A
lesser man would not."

"You give me too much credit, my dear."

She chuckled. "I do no such thing, sir. I have watched you
not only forgive the one who so grievously wronged you, but you
*have also taken care to ensure he knows that he is forgiven. **No***
mention of his wrongdoings has crossed your lips in his
***presence,"** she lifted a brow, "even when he has been particularly*
trying about something."

FINALLY MRS. DARCY, EPILOGUE

———

Though the wrongdoings and the pain which they caused
continue to exist as part of the backstory for *Finally Mrs. Dar-*
cy, according to Elizabeth's words in the passage above, Darcy is living out the truth of love "keeps no record of wrongs."
He has not allowed his anger and hurt to continue to bubble
below the surface as in the example of the co-worker at the
beginning of this post. He has laid it and Bingley's offense to
rest, never to be revisited again. And that is exactly what our

loving Heavenly Father does with our sin: He forgives it and never again brings it up as a charge against us.

For I will forgive their wickedness and will remember their sins no more. [*HEBREWS 8:12* NIV]

In acting in a way that is congruent with godly love, Darcy has re-established a friendship, ensured as happy a life for himself and Elizabeth as is humanly possible, gained a great deal of peace, and demonstrated clearly to all, who wish to take the time to notice, the strength and fortitude that true love demands.

6

REST EASY, MR. KELLET

♥

"HE SHOULD BE TOLD." She (Anne) began tracing circles on the back of Richard's hand with her free one. "He might rest easier if he knew." She drew in a deep, shaky breath. After a few moments of silence, she continued. "He made a promise to my father..." She drew in another shaky breath and shook her head.

"To protect you and your mother." Richard kissed the top of her head. "And he has done well. You are right; he should be told."

LISTEN TO YOUR HEART, CHAPTER 16

It is not only in the romantic relationship in my books where you can catch glimpses of God's love on display. It can be seen in familial relationships, friendships (as we saw in a previous journal entry), between a character and a stranger, and even between employer and employee, such as in the example that I want to briefly examine in this entry.

"It (love) always protects, always trusts, always hopes, always perseveres." [1 CORINTHIANS 13:7 NIV]

In *Listen to Your Heart,* danger abounds. The de Bourghs' estate, Rosings, has been the seat of great unrest and unhappiness for years and years. Alliances, murders, smuggling, and secrets colour every corner of the property. They slink and hide in the shadows until love and truth force them to show their scarred and heinous visages.

Yet, in the heart of this inhospitable climate, love survives and stands strong before erupting forth in new life.

Lovers who were separated in a horrific fashion are reunited. In the face of painful family divisions, as well as dire threats from without, relations stand united in pursuing the opportunity to marry as they choose. And a promise from a faithful servant to a good and kind master is fulfilled.

This faithful servant is Mr. Kellet, Rosings' butler. Like his master, Mr. Kellet was not born in England. He was born in France and came to serve Sir Louis de Bourgh, who was of noble birth, before Sir Louis escaped the troubles of the French Revolution. When Sir Louis escaped, he did not escape alone, and one of the people who came with him to England was Mr. Kellet.

Over the course of years, Mr. Kellet became more like a part of the family than just a mere servant. He stood guard over those in his household and kept careful watch to see that all the members of Sir Louis's family were kept as safe as could be. And at some point, before Sir Louis de Bourgh died, Mr. Kellet promised him that he would protect Anne and Lady Catherine.

———

"He must have the patience of Job to put up with Catherine as his employer," she (Lady Matlock) whispered to Richard. "The next master of Rosings will have a treasure in that man should he have the sense to retain Mr. Kellet. Your father tried to hire him away from Catherine, but Mr. Kellet would hear none of it. He

said he promised his master to look after the ladies of Rosings, and he is not a man to go back on his word. He keeps a close eye on things. If you ever need information on any who visit here, he is the person to see."

Richard's eyes grew wide at this information. "Indeed?"

She laughed softly, and her eyes twinkled. "How do you suppose I always knew what you and Darcy were up to when you were young?"

Richard shook his head. "I should have known you had a spy working for you." He opened the door to Anne's sitting room and allowed his mother to enter before him. Before she even spoke a word of greeting, she gathered Anne into her arms.

LISTEN TO YOUR HEART, CHAPTER 6

It was not a promise Mr. Kellet took lightly, nor it was one which would be fulfilled without great cost.

When Anne and her mother are at odds, Rosings' faithful butler is there keeping watch, assessing the dangers, and taking action to prevent injury and dispel the danger.

He is not, however, supernatural, and his love, care, and devotion to and for his master's family cannot be completely perfect. He is not able to anticipate or stop every evil plan. Though trouble arises and destroys, it will not prosper, for Mr. Kellet will not allow it. He will chase it down and rout it out.

Why?

Why would he not just attempt to mitigate the damage and be happy with that?

It's because of love. The love that Mr. Kellet has for the family he currently serves and the man he once called master will not allow him to leave his post as their guardian until he knows that they are well-protected. It is only when he is assured that he has fulfilled his duty and that his charges are safely under another's care that he can finally rest easy.

"You've served well. Sir Louis would be satisfied. I can take over from here." (Richard said)

Mr. Kellet took one last shallow breath, and Richard pulled Anne onto his lap where he held her while she wept.

LISTEN TO YOUR HEART, CHAPTER 16

That, my dear readers, is what godly love does. It protects to the end and in the face of great personal sacrifice.

"Greater love has no one than this: to lay down one's life for one's friends." [*JOHN 15:13* NIV]

7

Love's Quiet Assurance and Unbreakable Bonds

———— ❤ ————

"IF YOU COULD WAIT *but a year," she had said as they had strolled the perimeter of the ballroom last night, "then your inheritance will be yours."*

He had felt her hopefulness and had longed to be able to enter into it with her, but he knew the reality of the situation.

"He will not allow me to be free. He will insist on my marrying before he gives me one farthing more than I have," he had replied.

Her eyes had filled with tears that she had refused to shed, and his heart had broken a bit more at both the thought of a life without her and the knowledge that his father was the source of her pain.

"If I could wait," he had whispered, "I would wait a thousand years for you."

She had smiled sadly at him and said, "And I would wait for you."

He once again ran his gloved finger over the drawing in the pocket of his coat.

"Do not forget me," she had said as she had slipped it into his pocket when he was taking his leave of her.

He knew he would never forget her. He could not. She was burned into his heart forever.

HIS INCONVENIENT CHOICE, CHAPTER 1

———

Way back in the autumn of 2015, I started writing a series of four books which became *Choices, a Pride and Prejudice Variation Series.* The whole series starts with just one choice by a father, Mr. Bennet, to see his eldest two daughters happily married. The choice he makes to arrange a marriage through scheming leads to several other choices which, because I am writing romance, eventually lead to many happily ever afters.

The third book in that series is titled *His Inconvenient Choice.* In this book, a different sort of Colonel Fitzwilliam has fallen in love with Kitty Bennet. However, Kitty is not an heiress, nor does she have any significant connections. These things make her an unacceptable choice as far as the colonel's father is concerned.

This leaves us asking: What is love to do when faced with such opposition? Does it die away and become as if it never existed? Can it be transferred from one lady to another with ease or at all? Does it just cower in the shadows feeling bitter, ill-used, and unwilling to ever step into the light of day again?

Not in this story.

In this story, Kitty and the colonel's love demonstrates great strength, as well as hope and patience. Both are determined to find a way to overcome the seemingly insurmountable challenge placed before them, even if it takes years. The colonel decides to seek employment rather than counting on his inheritance. Kitty finds a way to also earn some money, which she hopes to use to help the colonel break free from his father's power.

———

Darcy stared at the door to Mrs. Havelston's shop for a moment. His aunt needed to know that her son was not the only one whose love was great. "She sold the designs for him," he said softly. "No one is supposed to know about the arrangement, so I am telling you in strictest confidence." He sighed. He knew that Miss Bingley and her friends would use the information, whether it was true or not, to disparage Kitty.

"What do you mean, she sold them for him? How would her selling designs assist Richard?"

"She spoke to me at Rycroft's wedding breakfast and asked me to invest the money she made from her sales. It was her hope that, someday, she would have enough set aside to help Richard do what he loves, and, perhaps, with any luck, she hoped he might still be free to marry her."

"But that would take years, would it not?" his aunt asked in surprise.

"She knew that." Darcy motioned to Lady Matlock's carriage. "It is time for me to go collect Richard."

She took his proffered arm. "Surely, Miss Bennet would marry, and the plan would come to naught. I cannot believe a husband would allow his wife to continue saving money for another man. No matter how noble the reason."

"She did not plan to marry if she could not marry Richard," he said as he handed his aunt into her carriage.

"But she is so young," Lady Matlock protested.

"And so very much in love," Darcy countered. "So very much in love," he repeated as he closed the door.

Things at this point in the story have turned from cloudy to downright dreary and appear utterly hopeless. The steps Kitty and Richard have taken to try to work out a solution to their predicament have fallen short – very short.

However, *"love always hopes, always perseveres."* [1 CORINTHI-ANS 13:7 NIV]

In this story, Kitty and the colonel are fortunate to have the support of a group of people who love them. These individuals step in when Kitty and Richard's world is darkest, and they work to dispel some of that darkness. While these individuals are doing their part, Kitty, who does not know what plans have been set in motion, sets out to make one final attempt at winning the colonel's freedom from his father – even if it comes at the cost of losing the man she loves.

"I must say I am impressed by my son's selection. You are lovely and daring, coming here to blackmail me with your sketches. Did you expect to win me over so that I would allow you to marry my son?"

Kitty groaned softly and rubbed her head. "I did not come to win the colonel's hand. I came to win his freedom."

"Freedom? I do not see how he has ever been anything but free."

She straightened herself and folded her hands primly in her lap, attempting to ignore the movement of the objects around her. His lordship was as ignorant as he was arrogant.

"My lord," she began in the most imposing tone she could muster, "if you will forgive me for being so direct, I must disagree. Neither man nor woman can be free when they are controlled by another. If you would but release him from his betrothal to his cousin and allow him to choose his own path..." She swallowed and allowed her gaze to drop. "I will give you my drawings and turn him away, if I must." She blinked at the tears that gathered.

HIS INCONVENIENT CHOICE, CHAPTER 19

But wait! Is this not love giving up hope and failing in an epic fashion?

No, this is love not being self-seeking [1 CORINTHIANS 13: 5 NIV].

I told you that Kitty and the colonel's love in this story was strong. Their love was never going to die. Their love was never going to give up hope – did you notice her small "if I must"? She still held a bit of hope in her heart, but this love was also not going to allow the object of her love to suffer if she could provide some relief, no matter the personal cost.

And because this is a work of fiction – and a romance at that! – with a sprinkling of writerly creativity and the help of a secret being revealed and an interesting advertisement in the paper, the patience, hope, and perseverance of Richard and Kitty's love will be rewarded as all good romances should be – with a very happy happily ever after.

Theirs was a love that would be spoken of in corners of drawing rooms and behind fans at balls, not for its passion, though there was plenty, nor for its demonstrative nature, though their hands were often joined in public, but for its quiet assurance and its unbreakable bonds.

8

From Distrust to Happily Ever After

"*I trust very few.*" *She trusted Bea and Mr. Clayton, as well as Mr. and Mrs. Shelton, and of course, Mr. Norman and – she nearly sighed – Walter. Perhaps it was more accurate to say she trusted all save her sister and anyone who appeared to love her sister. However, that would be rather rude to say, though the thought was tempting.*

"*No, you trust everyone,*" *Felicity countered.* "*You always have.*"

Grace shook her head. "*Not any longer.*"

HER SECRET BEAU, CHAPTER 15

Broken trust is a lot like a broken bottle of ink. As it spills out and covers all the surfaces in its path, the ink leaves a trail of potential destruction. Sometimes the mess the ink creates can be cleaned up easily, and the damage it causes can be mitigated. Often, however, it leaves behind indelible stains which alter forever the way something looks.

That's what has happened to Grace, the heroine of *Her Secret Beau*. You see, Grace was born with trust issues. Her personality is one that is given to trusting easily and eagerly. She is the sort who would think the best of everyone she met until she was told differently.

And do you know who has been telling her differently? Her older sister, Felicity.

Felicity is the creator of her own destiny. She's confident and possesses what could be wonderful leadership qualities if she were to point them in a proper direction. However, with Felicity's confidence has come a healthy dose of selfishness. According to her...

- She is the oldest sister.

- She should have the best.

- She is the one who should marry first.

- Her sister should do as she says.

- Even her friendships are a means to an end.

Have you ever met anyone like that? Unfortunately, I'm sure we all have.

Grace grew up trusting her sister and following naively in her shadow until Felicity went a step too far and broke the heart of a gentleman just because a better possibility for a husband (with a nicer house, bigger bank account, better career position) appeared on the scene.

From that point forward, Grace's ability to willingly and eagerly trust others begins to waver and causes her to take up a scheme to ensure her sister will not steal any other gentlemen from her. (Did I mention that Grace liked the gentleman whose heart got broken but had given him up because her sister claimed to love him? I didn't? Well, that happened.)

Much like Catherine Morland's story in *Northanger Abbey*, Grace's story, to this point in my *Touches of Austen* series, is a coming-of-age story. When we first meet her in book one of the series, she is naive. Then, in book two, she faces some harsh realities which shake her view of life. Finally, in book three, she steps out of the secondary character role and into the role of heroine and meets the gentleman who will help her learn that trusting is not as dangerous as it appears if one chooses to trust the right person. That right person is, of course, a person who loves Grace more than he loves himself.

"When I was a child, I thought like a child. I reasoned like a child. When I became a man, I put the ways of childhood behind me." [1 CORINTHIANS 13:11 NIV]

Along with learning who to trust in book three, Grace is also discovering that love is more than just a game a lady plays to score the handsomest husband with the best estate and bank account. She is in the process of putting away childish things and putting on more mature ideas and thoughts.

And Mr. Walter Blakesley, who is book three's trustworthy hero – despite his willingness to partake in Grace's scheme to deceive her sister and mother – is just the person to help Grace learn about love.

————

A pained expression created a great furrow between Grace's eyes. "Then, how is one ever to know if one is in love enough to marry?"

"That is an excellent question," Roger replied, turning to Walter. "Do you have an explanation? You always had some reply when we pondered such impossible things in school."

Walter shook his head. "I am afraid my answer will not be satisfying, for I think that love is not something which can be dissected into bits and pieces to be analyzed for proof of existence. Not that it cannot be examined and found to exist."

"I am terribly confused," Grace said.

Walter smiled at her. "I think that one just simply knows, and that, for each person, the item of proof differs despite some similarities in all cases."

HER SECRET BEAU, CHAPTER 10

For Grace, that item of proof comes in the form of Walter's refusal to ask Felicity to dance, which causes her to realize, as her scheme is falling apart, that Mr. Blakesley was right.

"...I will remind you, however, that your sister will never sway me to pay her any particular attention."

"I cannot trust her," Grace said softly.

"You do not have to. You need only trust me."

HER SECRET BEAU, CHAPTER 11

Grace's trust did not need to be in her sister, who, at this point in the story, is still a selfish creature. Her trust only needed to rest in Walter and his love for her above all others.

"That was my promise," he said. "And I will never break a promise I have made to you. Even if I found your sister charming – which I do not – I would not break it."

HER SECRET BEAU, CHAPTER 16

Of course, just when Grace has realized that she can trust Walter, just when she's finally ready to allow him to tell the world he is courting her, just as she is facing a delightfully happy future free from fear of her sister's machinations, her newly claimed loved is put to the test.

1 Corinthians 13:7 says that love "always protects, always trusts, always hopes, always perseveres." You'll notice that

trust is included in a list of related qualities here that follow a natural progression.

Remember how I said that Walter was going to help Grace learn about love? Let me summarize how Walter has, and will, live out the progression of love found in the above verse.

To begin with in *Her Secret Beau*, Grace witnessed Walter's protection. In this case, the protection is not from anything life-threatening or excessively dangerous, but it is rather protection from a scheming sister, which, to Grace, is a very important thing from which to be shielded. Remember, her sister has broken her trust. That stain has darkened Grace's view of the world and threatens to make her future quite bleak. Walter's steadfast, honest character is just the balm that is needed to keep Grace from falling completely into despair and distrust.

As a result of Walter's actions in proving his willingness to keep her heart from being broken by her sister, Grace has opened her heart to trusting and loving him. Then, when things become grim and as Grace attempts to protect him, Walter will complete the progression of love. For, instead of giving up when presented with less than favourable circumstances, he will cling to hope and determinedly pursue a happy resolution.

And, though this story is set in a fictional world and is played out by imperfectly perfect characters, is that not a lovely picture of what love should be? Protecting, trusting, hoping, and persevering.

"We are ready," Walter said.

"Ready for what?" Grace batted her lashes at him innocently, causing him to chuckle.

"Feigned innocence will not work with me, Mrs. Blakesley. I know you are very good at scheming. The only way to discover this secret is to follow me."

"Anywhere."

"I could be leading you into danger," he cautioned.

Grace rolled her eyes. "You would never do that."

"Are you certain?"

She nodded. There was no one, absolutely no one, whom she trusted more than the man standing before her.

9

Unfailing Love: Beauty Amid the Bleakness

Love never fails. But where there are prophecies, they will cease; where there are tongues, they will be stilled; where there is knowledge, it will pass away.

1 Corinthians 13:8 NIV

I don't know the number of times I have seen some wall hanging or meme that bears the words "Love Never Fails." It's probably one of the most familiar sentences from the Bible's "Love Chapter" (1 Corinthians 13). And while it is a wonderful statement, what follows that portion of 1 Corinthians 13:8 is what makes it perhaps the most beautiful sentence in the chapter, for it is in the rest of the verse that we see the illustration of what never-failing means.

Do you see it? Prophecies will stop. Tongues will fall silent. Knowledge will be no more. But even when everything is gone, love will still remain. I think that image of everything falling away and love standing there, all alone, in the bleakness is just beautiful. And that is what we are going to talk about in this journal entry.

In my book *His Irreplaceable Belle*, which is book four in my *Touches of Austen* series, everything seems to have fallen away. Hope no longer colours the hero and heroine's worlds very brightly. It might give a faint hue of pleasantness for their future – a state of being content with second best – but it no longer splashes on vibrant hues of delight or great joy. That's because the characters and plot for this book have been touched by Jane Austen's *Persuasion*.

As any good Jane Austen fan will know, Persuasion is a second-chance romance in which the main love interests are separated for a period of years and, when reunited, do not immediately profess their love for each other, but eventually come together in the end.

So, too, in my book, the main characters have been separated.

Six years before the beginning of the story, the hero was deemed unworthy of the heroine, and the heroine was persuaded away from marrying the hero. However, the circumstances surrounding these facts differ in my story from what Miss Austen wrote.

———

He (Fritz) was a gentleman who, quite naturally, felt compelled to see to the needs of everyone, and whose compulsion to care for others only intensified when presented with the needs of someone counted among those whom he held dear. It was this caring and compassionate part of his nature which had first drawn Belle to him and had recommended him to her as a gentleman with a promising future. He had not had much in the way of wealth and worldly possessions when they had first met, but she had known, to the depths of her soul, that it was only a temporary state for him. She had always believed he would be a great success, and from what she had seen today and had heard since she arrived in Bath, her assessment had been correct. He was a success and would continue to be so.

Oh, to be a part of his life and cheer him on to further greatness as his wife! Her heart still cried for what had been lost. It ached with its desire to be the lady at his side. But how could she be? Why would a gentleman who had been so wronged ever wish to be tied to the very family who had threatened to deny him of his profession?

His Irreplaceable Belle, Chapter 2

———

Fritz, as a young physician's assistant, had found himself on the wrong side of Belle's father and oldest brother simply by falling in love. Neither approved of Belle wasting her beauty by marrying someone of little means and low standing. Not only did they disapprove and were unwilling to consent to the relationship, but they also took it a step further and attempted to destroy Fritz's career.

Fritz finds himself pushed out from the society he knew to find his way in a new place and without the lady he loves. He throws himself into his work and becomes exactly what Belle thought he would be – a great success. He does not become who he is at the beginning of our story on his own, however.

———

For the next several minutes, Fritz enjoyed the weaving and circling of the dance as he watched Miss James complete the patterns with a word here and there passing between her and Mrs. Blakesley when possible. They seemed to be forming a fine acquaintance. This was also a good thing as Fritz could not countenance taking a wife who might separate him from Walter.

Walter had been the first close acquaintance that Fritz had made in Bath. Fritz had been here for two years, establishing himself as a physician before he had met Walter when Walter had fallen ill with a fever. It had not been a serious illness, just enough of one to require some advice for regaining health. The meeting had been as much of a balm to Fritz's soul as his tinctures and recipe for barley water had been to Walter.

Walter had healed quickly, and then, he had provided his own sort of healing to Fritz. It was Walter who had taught him that there were still people in the world who were trustworthy and loyal and who were opposed to carrying tales and viewing themselves as better than everyone else. They had been fast friends ever since. Fritz could not give up such a relationship. He simply could not. Therefore, he was excessively pleased when upon the completion of their set of dances, Miss James invited the Blakesleys to meet her mother and aunt.

HIS IRREPLACEABLE BELLE, CHAPTER 7

You may remember Walter Blakesley from a previous journal entry. He is the hero of Her Secret Beau where he teaches Grace about the trustworthiness of love. In this story, he has provided the same service to his best friend, and in so doing, he has helped Fritz heal and thrive, despite his broken heart. Throughout His Irreplaceable Belle, Walter will continue to be a solid support for Fritz and will be instrumental in eventually bringing Belle and Fritz together.

But I shouldn't allow myself to get too sidetracked here. I wanted to focus on the romantic relationship not the friendship relationships in this story (although those friendships are well-worth a study.)

While Fritz has become a well-respected and sought-after physician in Bath – one of the best (unless you ask Walter who will declare him THE best) – he still suffers from a broken heart. He is not alone in this. Belle also bears a broken heart.

She has long regretted having been persuaded by her mother's tears to refuse Fritz's offer to run away and marry in Scotland. At the beginning of our story, her father has finally given up hope that she will ever marry and, at her aunt's request, has sent her to live with her Aunt Augusta in Bath.

Both Fritz and Belle attempt to settle into life without the other, but it is no use. It cannot be done, and in the end, as one might suspect in a romance, they finally find their happily ever after. However, as I always say...

> *Happily ever after doesn't mean perfect. Even*
> *fairytale princesses have scars.*

When the curtain drops on *His Irreplaceable Belle*, the atrocities and disapproval of the past do not magically drop away. Instead, Belle and Fritz will find themselves holding on to each other and standing victorious over the bleakness that had once been their lot in life, and proving that, despite the scars and all that was lost, it can truly be said that "love never fails."

10

No Greater Love

---♥---

SHE HAD JUST RUINED herself. How was she to find acceptance and a husband of any worth if she were to be shunned? She knew very well how vicious Sarah could be.

"Miss Crawford, the cannons will run their course, and when the smoke clears, you will have your prize. Do you know what that prize is?" He shot an angry glare at Tom while speaking gently to her.

She shook her head.

He took her hand. "You will have destroyed the admiral."

Mary blinked.

"You will have destroyed the admiral," Gabe repeated.

She nodded as a skitter of excitement danced up her arms, causing them to shiver. She would like nothing better than to destroy every trace of the admiral who had found his way into her behaviour.

"We..." He shot another glare at Tom. "...will not let you take on water."

———————

At the beginning of book 3 in my *Other Pens* series, Mary Crawford finds herself at a crossroads.

Because of her selfish behaviour, she finds herself cut off from her brother.

Because of what Tom Bertram talks to her about in the garden at a soiree, she sees herself for what she is.

And then, she finds she must make a choice because she accepted a dance with a tradesman – one who had gained much of his wealth through privateering no less!

What are the two life paths that converge at this crossroads for Miss Crawford?

She must choose either to continue as she has been, which would please her friends who have led her down a destructive road, or to cut ties with them, form new friendships, and remould herself into someone that she can like.

So what does she choose?

Notice the excerpt above. In that bit of story, we learn two things about Mary.

First, we know which choice she made. It was the hardest of the two choices which stood before her, but it was the best choice, even if at the moment where the excerpt begins, she is just realizing how damaging her choice could be to her place in society.

Second, the excerpt also tells us what she does not want to be but has become – someone who is very much like her uncle, the admiral.

Mary, unfortunately, grew up with horrible examples of what adults should be like. Her aunt and uncle (aka the admiral), with whom she and her brother lived for years, were constantly attempting to manipulate each other. To the admiral, women were only really good for one thing – his pleasure. But then, everyone, male or female, was only considered good to the admiral if they could help him in some way. He was not one to be trusted, nor was he one to even pretend to be kind.

Mary's friends were of the same bent as her aunt and uncle – they were only truly looking out for themselves. Pleasure was their prize, but it never really satisfied. In fact, it kept them searching for more and always hoping that the next enjoyable thing would quench their desires.

That's not a very loving environment in which to grow up or live! Therefore, Mary has very little understanding of what true love is, and her trust in men is lacking even more than her understanding of love is.

Happily for her, I'm telling her story and have allowed her to find just the right sort of fellow to show her what an honourable, trust-him-with-your-life man is.

That man, Gabriel Durward, may be fearsome to those who dare to cross him, but he is also loyal and good to those who are his friends. He is a man of his word and as trustworthy as any could be. When he makes a promise, it's not going to be broken while he lives.

Gabe began his life in India, where his father was working for the East India Company. For a time, he worked on some of the East India Company's ships, but then, he decided to strike out on his own. He has captained a few privateers in his day and now invests in privateers and deals in reselling the cargo he buys at prize auctions. His father is no longer living, and so his mother, who is from India, has come to live in London with him.

While he might not have gotten on perfectly well with his father, his father still loved him and treated him well. And his mother, well, she loves him fiercely and extends that same sort of care to all her son's friends. He is the apple of her eye, but then, he loves her as dearly as she loves him. It is from her that he has inherited the trait of stalwartly caring for his friends.

As Gabe and Mary's story plays out, and each falls more and more in love with the other, Mary's former friends are not happy to have lost her friendship and attempt to discredit Gabe. Added to that bit of trouble, Gabe has an enemy of his own from the past who is also determined to do him harm.

Mary ends up in the middle of all this mess, and her fledgling bravery in deciding to trust Gabe is tested and threatens to break her heart when her friends spread malicious tales about him. However, the pain those tales have the ability to bring is nothing compared to the sorrow she will feel if Gabe's enemy is successful.

It is in the middle of this mess where Mary discovers just how trustworthy Gabe is. In the excerpt above, he has promised to *not let her take on water*. It's his way of saying that he will do whatever it takes to protect her – even to the point of giving his life to do so.

———

Mr. Durward grasped her hand. "You are safe now."

She nodded as tears filled her eyes.

He smiled once more before his eyes fluttered closed and did not reopen. Mary fell on his chest once more. Her tears soaked his jacket as she listened for a heartbeat. It was there, but it was not strong.

"Please," she pleaded. "Do not die."

"Miss."

"Crawford," Margaret said. "And I am Mrs. Grant, her sister."

"Mr. Waller, one of Mr. Durward's partners," Mary heard whoever it was that had joined them say.

"It will take some time to get this ship back to the quay. If you are not afraid to do so, you can return to the shore in the rowboat with Mr. Durward. It is a faster way to travel."

"Miss Crawford?" Mr. Waller crouched near her. "Does he live?"

MARY: TO PROTECT HER HEART, CHAPTER 14

———

If Mr. Waller knew that this was a romance story (and not just a love story), he'd know that there had to be a happy ending for Mary and Gabe. It's really too bad that not even Mary knew that at this point in the story, for I'm sure it would have been quite a balm to her spirit to have known at this moment that he would survive.

But neither Mr. Waller nor Mary know that a happy ending is coming. For them, it appears as if a tragic end is a very real outcome.

Thinking about that, imagine how Jesus's friends and disciples must have felt when he was led out to be crucified and when his lifeless body was laid in the grave. They didn't know what we know. They didn't know that He would rise from that grave. He had told them he would, but they hadn't understood what he was saying.

"Greater love has no one than this: to lay down one's life for one's friends." [JOHN 15:13 NIV]

I rather doubt that Mary knew this Bible verse, but I can guarantee you that she knew the truth of it when Gabe finally declared his love for her.

"You are my heart," Gabe said when she looked up from the beautiful ring to his face. "And I would give my very life to see you safe and happy."

Her lips quivered as happy tears gathered in her eyes. "You already have, or at least, you attempted to."

"I would do it again," he said as he stroked a finger along her cheek. "I need no warehouses, no business deals, no prize ships, or their bounty to be happy, Mary. I need only you, for you are my prize of greatest value. Please say you will be my wife."

MARY: TO PROTECT HER HEART, CHAPTER 16

There was no doubt left in her mind about how trustworthy her future husband was. There was no worry that he might try to manipulate her against her will or treat her poorly. She didn't just have faith that he would protect her. She didn't just hope that he would protect her. She knew with every bit of her being that Gabriel Durward loved her, and his love was of the greatest kind. The kind of love which would always do whatever was within its power to protect her.

> *"And now these three remain: faith, hope, and love. But the greatest of these is love."* [1 CORINTHIANS 13:12 NIV]

Ah, yes! The greatest of these truly is love.

11

THE MOST IMPORTANT PART

"ARE YOU READY TO introduce the world to the Miss Darcy I see and love?" Alfred held his hand out to her.

"I think I am." There was a little fizzing of nerves in her stomach, but it was not unbearable at all.

"All will be well," he assured her as she placed her hand in his.

And she knew it would be, for how could it be anything but wonderful when she had Alfred at her side? Her free hand touched the pendant of her necklace, and she knew that beneath it, her heart was and always would be safe for it had chosen to love a good man.

Alfred cocked an eyebrow in question.

She smiled. "I am ready, my love. Lead on."

And with a squeeze of her hand and a whispered "I love you," he did just that, leading her to the door of the assembly room and stepping into a future filled not only with dances and dinner parties but also with an abundance of love and joy.

_____

When you read a romance, where do you start?

If you're like many, you look at that question and think, "Um, at the beginning," while giving me one of those looks that says I might have something wrong with me if I don't know that.

However, if you're anything like me, the answer to that question is not automatically evident because I don't always start reading at the beginning. In fact, I begin most books by reading the best part, aka the ending, first.

I can hear some of you gasp in horror because you would find that reading the ending first "spoils" the story. But for me, it doesn't.

For me, the ending of the story is the most important part.

It's that last chapter of the story which determines if I am going to invest time into reading the book or not. If the story is a cliffhanger or doesn't satisfactorily conclude with a happily ever after, I discard that book and pick up another. If the ending is "ok," meaning it has the two people together and happy, but it feels a little emotionless or flat when reading, I might read the rest of the book, or I might shelve it until later.

When I read the ending, I want that final chapter to make me curious about how these two got to where they are. I want it to leave me with that wonderful feeling of having savoured a special treat. I want it to whisper, "Read more," and to make me hope for an epilogue or to see this couple again in another book in the series. I want it to fill me with hope and joy that the two imaginary characters who have found a place in my heart will continue to stand strong together in their love. I want that everlasting, never-ending feeling.

If the ending of the book promises to give me that, then, I'm eager to read the rest of the book (because we all know that endings are best enjoyed when the beginning and middle have built up to them, right?).

Let's take the example of the ending from *Protecting Miss Darcy* that I shared above and consider how I would evaluate it.

First, these lines tell me that our couple, Miss Darcy and Alfred, are happily in love, and I can just begin to feel that emotional connection.

Next, these lines also let me know that their future will be together and happy.

And then, these lines leave me with some questions, including: What was the fear she overcame? What happened that caused her to feel unsafe? Is there something special about that pendant? Is that why she touches it? and What makes him a good man?

These questions would then beg me to discover the answers, and I'd be off and reading – sometimes from the beginning and sometimes working my way backward through the book. (Yes, I know that's odd.)

Now, let's look at how 1 Corinthians 13 ends.

> *For now we see only a reflection as in a mirror; then we shall see face to face. Now I know in part; then I shall know fully, even as I am fully known. And now these three remain: faith, hope and love. But the greatest of these is love.* [1 CORINTHIANS 13:11-12 NIV]

When I read that final verse, it feels like a satisfying conclusion. Three things remain – they haven't been destroyed or annihilated – and the greatest of them is love. Love stands above all the rest. I think that's pretty awesome and quite satisfying.

But when I read that last verse and the one right before it, I'm left with some questions: When will we see face to face? What are we seeing face to face? Why is what we have only a reflection? What does it mean I will fully know, even as I am fully known? and Why, or how, is love the greatest?

To find answers to those questions, you're going to have to read more than just one chapter of the Bible. In fact, to understand the answers to those questions best, you might want to read the whole Bible – yes, even the Old Testament, for it, too, points to Christ.

And just like the ending of a romance story is best enjoyed when the beginning and middle have been read, so, too, it is with the Scriptures. There are no extraneous parts. The beginning, the middle, and the end all come together to tell the tale of history and eternity. There are good guys and bad guys, evil plots and acts of redemption. There is regular life and how it gets lived. There are descriptions of various settings and people. And through it all is woven a thread of love from even before the first sin occurs to well after the last sin is committed. From the ruining of Eden to its restoration, love – real, true, godly love – is at the heart of God's story about His relationship with you and me.

God's story isn't done. The conclusion has not been written in the annals of history just yet. It's still in the future. We can read about the conclusion in several books of prophecy. God has revealed to us something of what will happen.

Though those prophecies can leave us guessing as to when the end will be and how it will unfold, we can be assured of one thing: God's love never fails, and when the pages of the history of this world or our lives close, His love will still remain. For those who have placed their faith and hope in Christ, love will greet them in an eternity that, like the future predicted in the story excerpt at the beginning of this journal entry, will be filled with an abundance of joy.

And now, wouldn't you agree that an ending like that is truly the best and most important part of the whole story?

As We Part for Now

AND SO WE COME to the conclusion of this brief writer's journal about how God's love shows up in the romances I write, and honestly, I feel almost guilty that I have only shared eleven short glimpses with you when I know that there are so many more woven through the pages of the many stories I have written. I'm positive that each of the characteristics of love listed in 1 Corinthians 13 could have been illustrated many times over by different books, but then, that might become boring, and one must know when to say, "Enough."

It is my hope that you have enjoyed these journal entries and that they have helped you glimpse God's love in places where it might not be expected. It is also my hope that reading this journal has given you some time and space to meditate on His love.

"For now we only see a reflection as in a mirror, then we shall see face to face." [1 CORINTHIANS 13:11 NIV]

I know that the plot points and characters written in my books are just shimmering, dim reflections of the real thing, and anything that my characters have done pales nearly to non-existence when held up against what God had done for us.

"For God so loved the world that he gave his one and only Son, that whoever believes in him shall not perish but have eternal life." [JOHN 3:16 NIV]

Be that as it may, I do believe that the stories highlighted in this journal stand as good illustrations of what we are to do and how we are to interact with those around us. I don't know how it is for you, but for me, having a mental picture of what an abstract term such as *godly love* looks like helps me to understand and remember it.

It is, therefore, my hope that perhaps the imaginary friends I share with you in my stories and this journal will come to mind from time to time and help you to do as the Apostle Paul instructs us in Ephesians 5 – walk in the way of love.

"Follow God's example, therefore, as dearly loved children and walk in the way of love, just as Christ loved us and gave himself up for us as a fragrant offering and sacrifice to God." [EPHESIANS 5:1-2 NIV]

Thank you for spending your time reading my thoughts about God's love and the blessing He has given me to write romances.

Until next time,

May God's love shine in, on, and through you.

Leenie

If you enjoyed this book, be sure to let others know by leaving a review.

~*~*~

Want to know when other Leenie books will be available?

You can always know what's new with my books by subscribing to my mailing list.

leeniebrown.com/subscribe

About Leenie

Leenie Brown has always been a girl with an active imagination, which, while growing up, was both an asset, providing many hours of fun as she played out stories, and a liability, when her older sister and aunt would tell her frightening tales. At one time, they had her convinced Dracula lived in the trunk at the end of the bed she slept in when visiting her grandparents!

Although it has been years since she cowered in her bed in her grandparents' basement, she still has an imagination which occasionally runs away with her, and she feeds it now as she did then — by reading!

Her heroes, when growing up, were authors, and the worlds they painted with words were (and still are) her favourite playgrounds! Now, as an adult, she spends much of her time in the Regency world, playing with the characters from her favourite Jane Austen novels and those of her own creation.

When she is not traipsing down a trail in an attempt to keep up with her imagination, Leenie resides in the beautiful province of Nova Scotia with her two sons and her very own Mr. Brown (a wonderful mix of all the best of Darcy, Bingley, and Edmund with a healthy dose of the teasing Mr. Tilney and just a dash of the scolding Mr. Knightley).

More Books by Leenie

You can find all of Leenie's books at this link

bit.ly/LeenieBBooks
where you can explore the collections below
~*~

Dash of Darcy and Companions Collection

Marrying Elizabeth Series

Sweet Possibilities and Sweet Extras

Willow Hall Romances

The Choices Series

Darcy Family Holidays

Darcy and... An Austen-Inspired Collection

Teatime Tales (Sweet Austen-inspired Novelettes)

Other Pens

Touches of Austen

Nature's Fury and Delights (Sweet Regency Novelettes)

Connect with Leenie

Mailing List: leeniebrown.com/subscribe
Website: *leeniebrown.com*
Patreon: patreon.com/LeenieBrown
Facebook: facebook.com/LeenieBrownAuthor
MeWe: mewe.com/p/leeniebrown1
Instagram: @leeniebbooks
E-mail: *LeenieBrownAuthor@gmail.com*